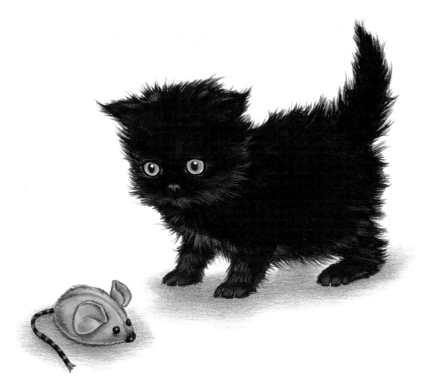

Draw and Color
Cats & Kittens

Learn to draw and color 26 different
kitties, step by easy step,
shape by simple shape!

Illustrated by Diana Fisher

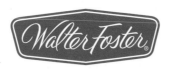

WalterFoster®

Getting Started

When you **look** closely at the **drawings** in this book, you'll notice that they're made up of basic shapes, such as circles, triangles, and rectangles. To draw all your favorite felines, just start with simple shapes as you see here. It's easy and fun!

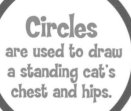

Circles are used to draw a standing cat's chest and hips.

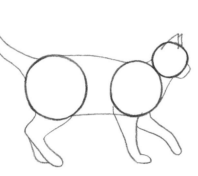

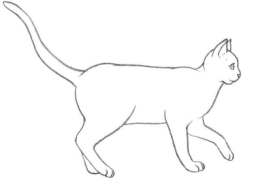

Ovals are good for starting out a seated feline.

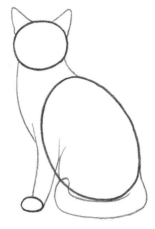

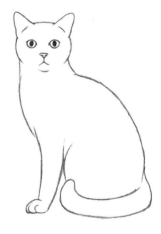

Triangles are purr-fect for most cats' ears.

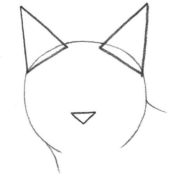

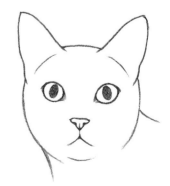

Coloring Tips

There's more than one way to bring your **fave felines** to life on paper—you can use crayons, markers, or colored pencils. Just be sure you have plenty of good natural colors, such as black, brown, orange, pink, and green.

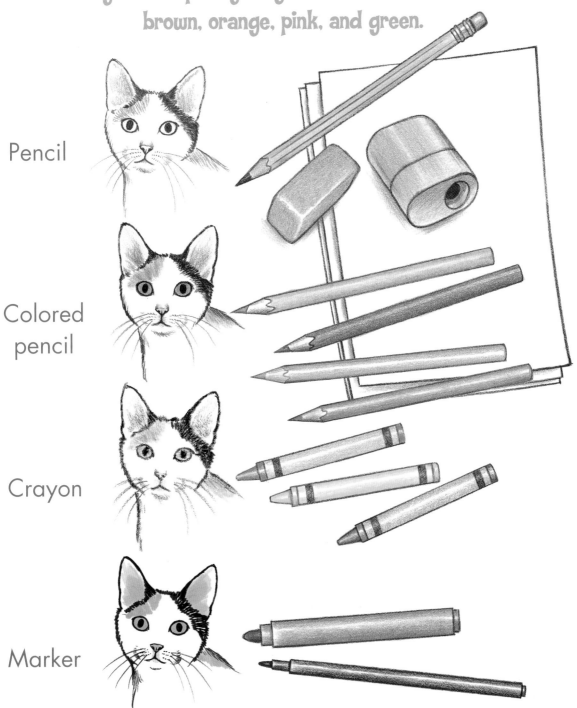

Pencil

Colored pencil

Crayon

Marker

Persian Cat

The **popular** Persian is known for its **long,** luxurious coat. But its face, neck, body, and legs are all short—as is its bushy tail!

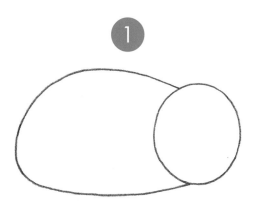

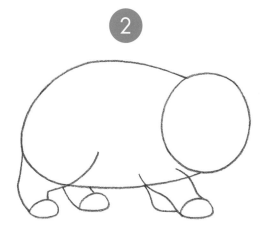

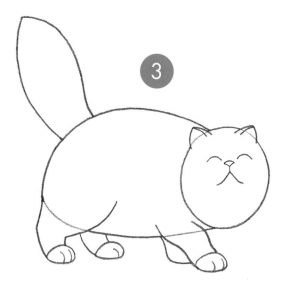

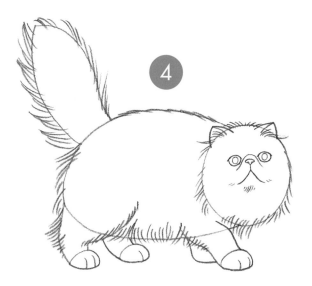

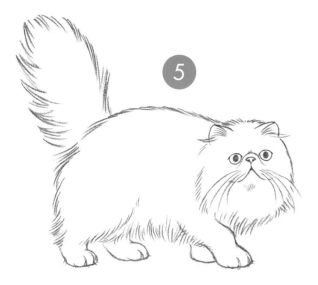

5

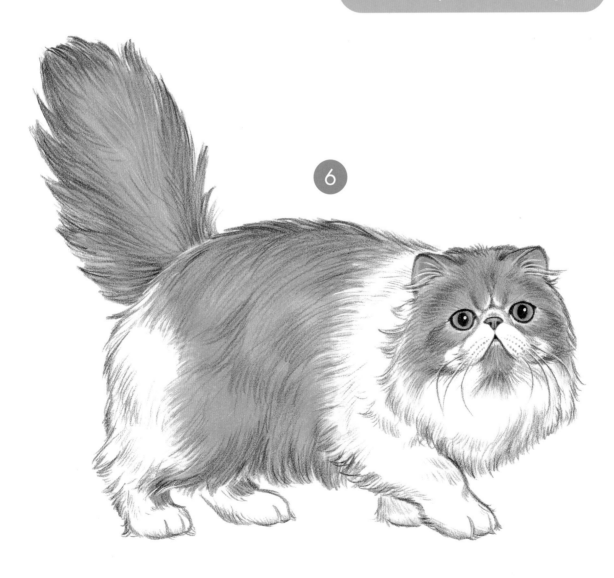

6

Egyptian Mau

The Mau cat sports both **spots** and **stripes!** And this social kitty has a reputation for being playful as well as graceful.

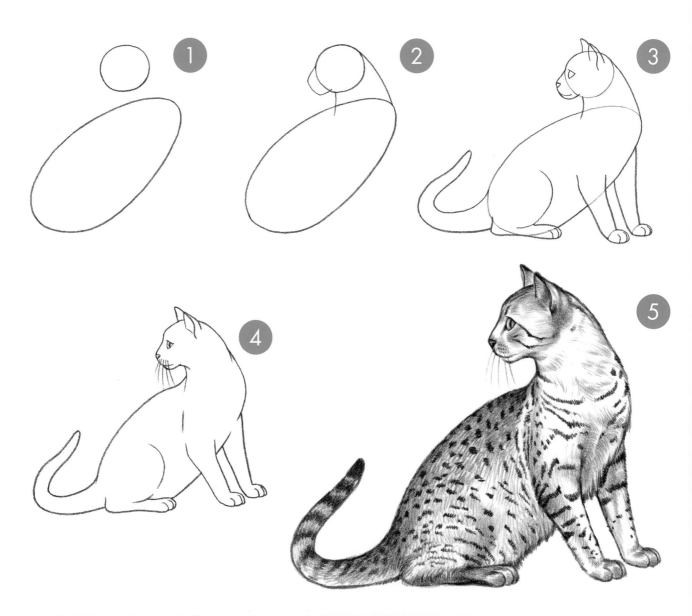

1
2
3
4
5

fun fact At one point in time, people were not allowed to take cats out of Egypt. But a Russian princess was able to use her social connections to do just that. She bred the cats and named the new breed *Mau*—the Egyptian word for cat.

British Shorthair

The best words to describe this feline are **large** and **round!**
And circles and ovals are the purr-fect shapes for drawing this quiet cat!

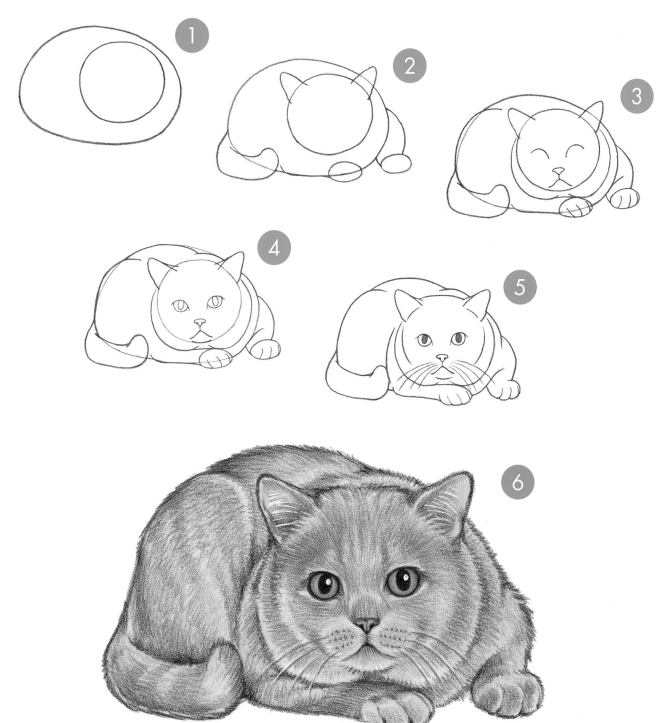

Selkirk Rex Kitten

Selkirk Rex kittens often have **shaggy,** rumpled-looking **fur.**
When they reach adulthood, their wavy locks become curly coats.

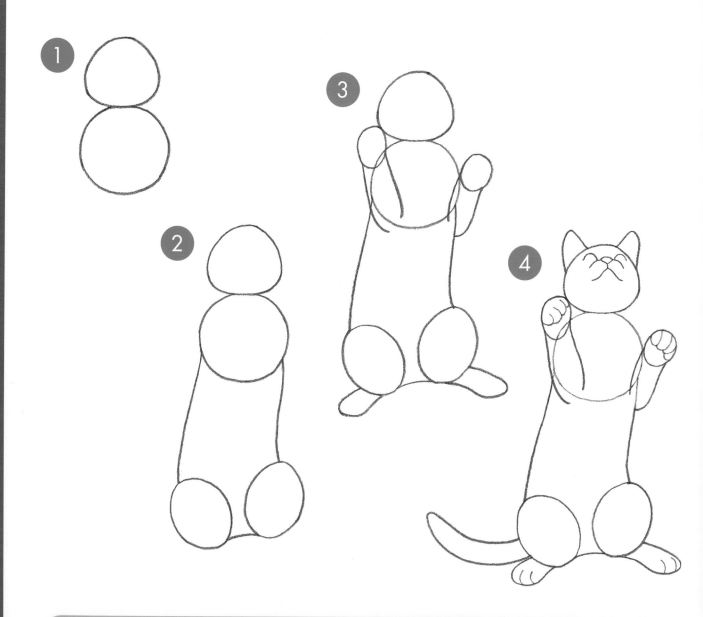

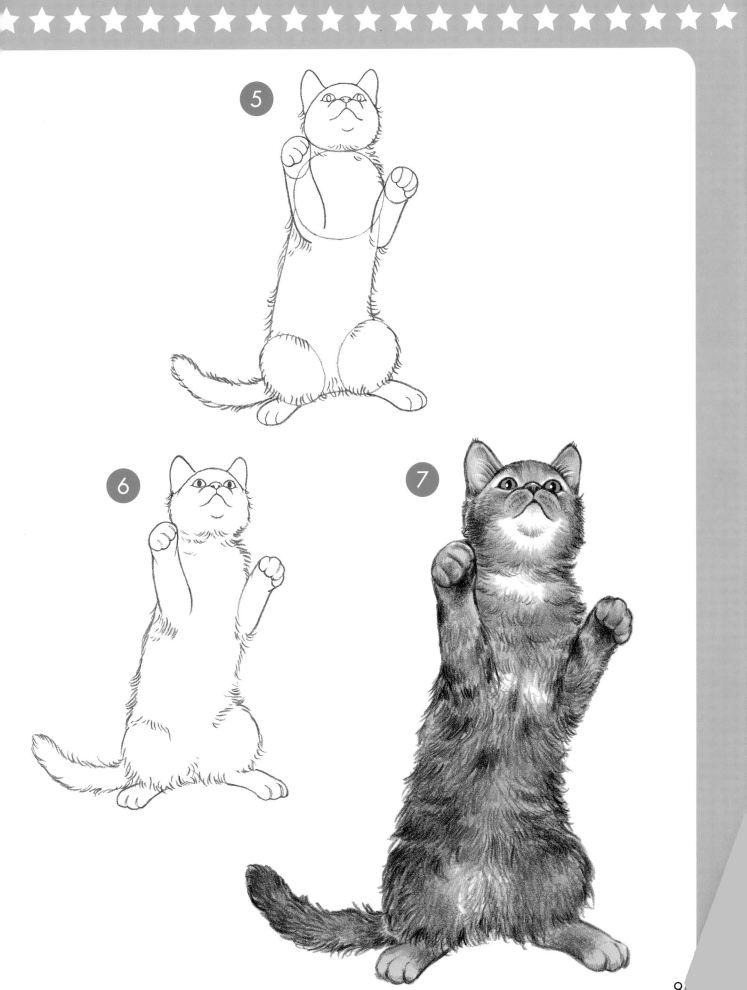

Abyssinian Kitten

Abys are short-haired cats with **strong** bodies—and stronger personalities! These curious kitties are intelligent and outgoing.

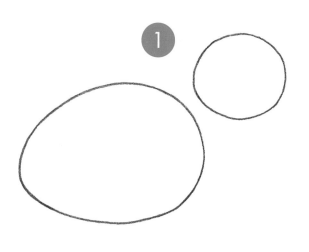

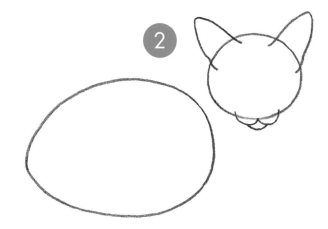

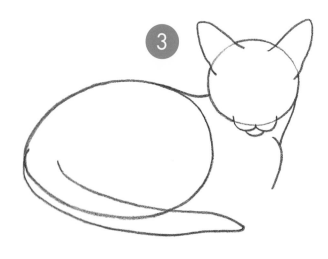

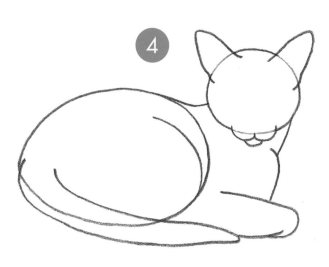

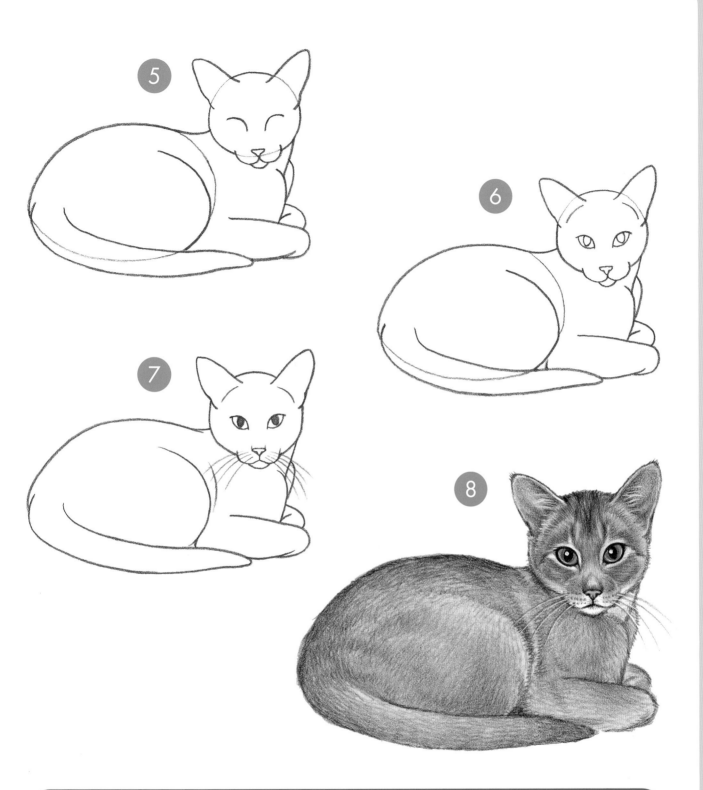

fun fact

The first documented Aby came from Ethiopia in 1868—but many believe that this elegant breed is a descendant of the cats of ancient Egypt! The mummified cats found in Pharaohs' tombs are similar to today's Abyssinian in many ways.

Ocicat

Despite its large, **muscular** body, the **spotted** Ocicat is graceful. This exotic-looking tabby has a long tail that tapers to a point.

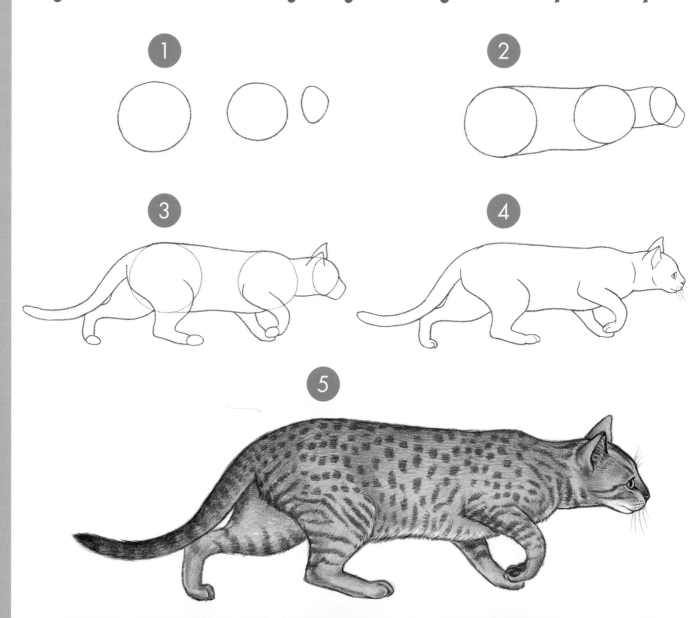

1

2

3

4

5

fun fact The Ocicat has markings similar to the ocelot, a South American wild cat. But its markings take time to develop. Ocicat kittens have solid stripes along their backs; these lines of dark color separate into spots as the cats age!

Persian Himalayan Kitten

This **snuggly** ball of **fur** is a special kind of Persian. It has a "color point" pattern, with darker shading on its tail, legs, ears, and face.

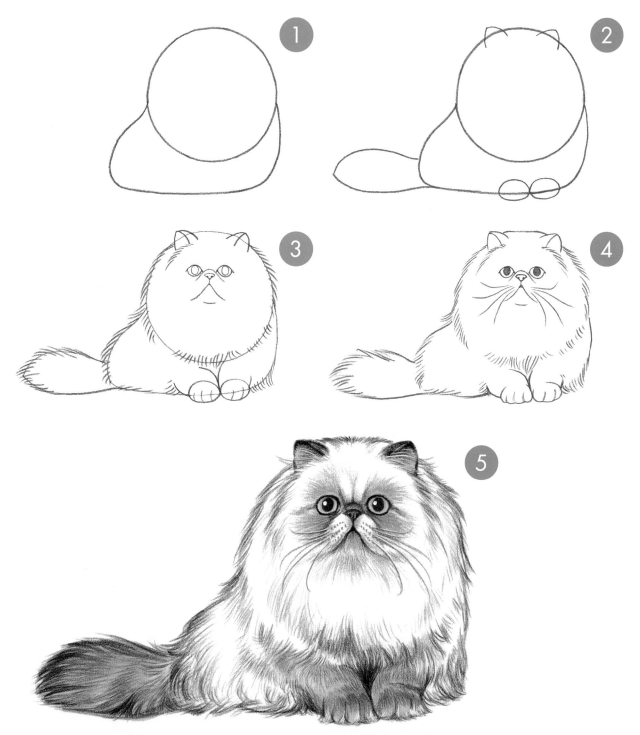

Cornish Rex

With a **wavy** coat, a **wiry** body, a whiplike tail, and prominent "bat" ears, the Cornish Rex is easy to notice and hard to forget!

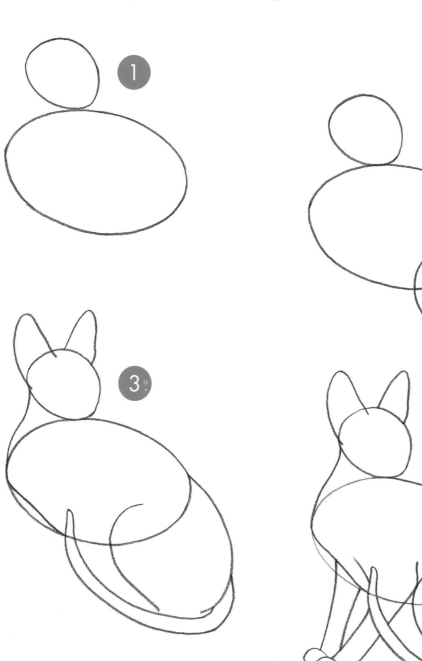

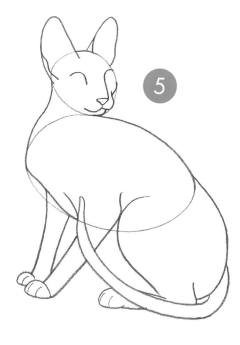

5

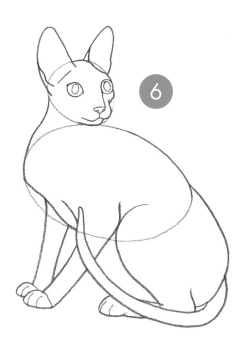

6

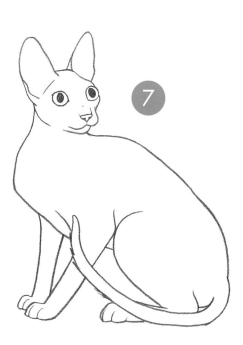

7

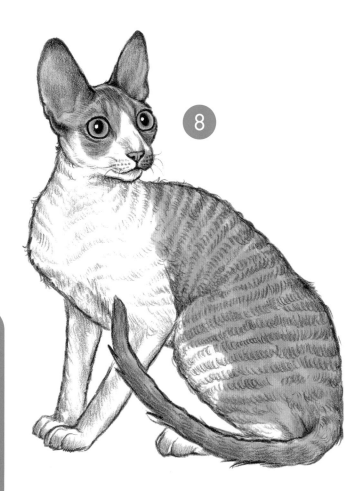

8

Maine Coon

It's easy to see where the **gentle giant** of the cat world got its name! This Maine native has a bushy, ringed tail—like a raccoon's!

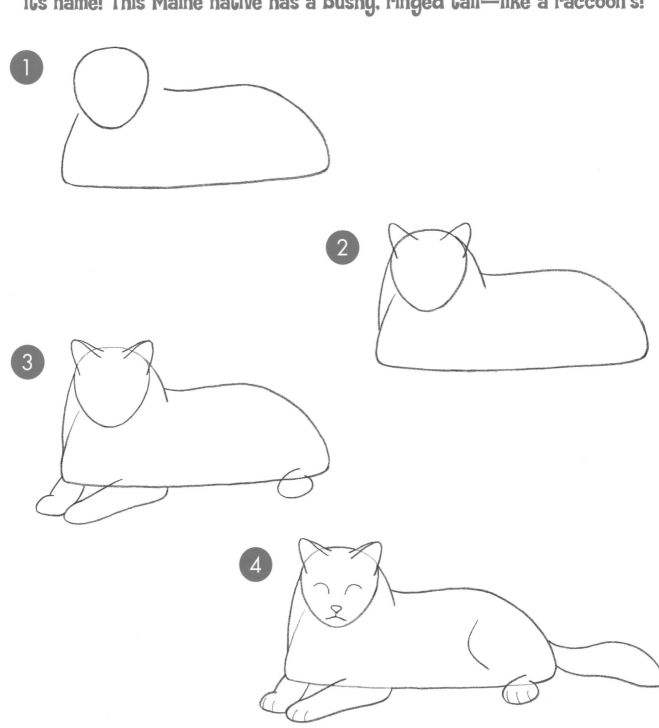

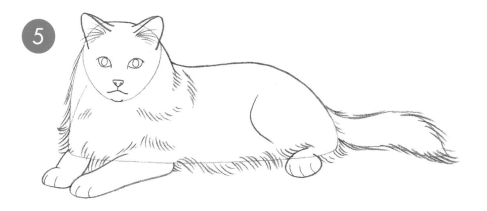

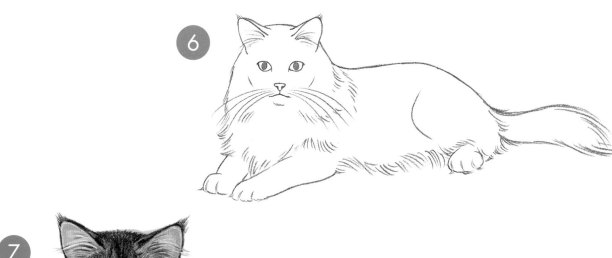

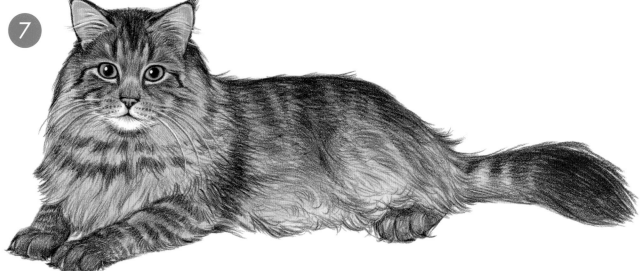

fun fact

The Maine Coon is the oldest American breed and the first native American show cat! Although it now places second in breed popularity, the Coon comes first in size. Some males weigh 20 pounds or more, and this Yankee cat is four times the size of the Singapura, the smallest cat breed.

Ragdoll

This soft, **fluffy** cat is so relaxed that it **flops** like a rag doll when picked up! An affectionate breed, Ragdolls love to cuddle.

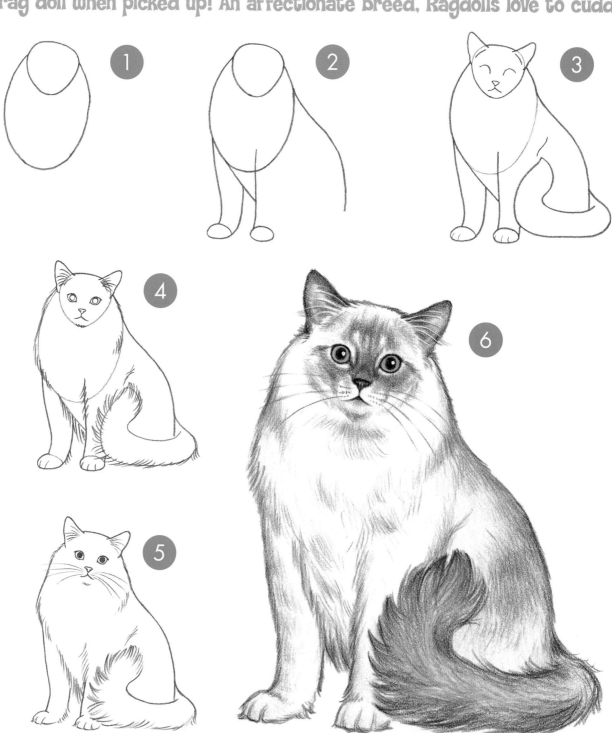

Manx

The Manx is a **mouser** with only a small **bump** for a tail! And with its longer rear legs, this kitty shows off its "rumpy riser."

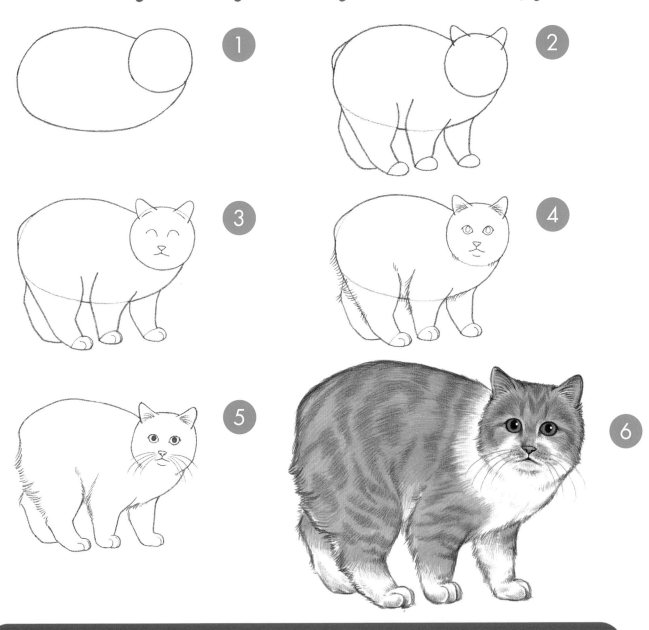

Curious Kittens

Cats have a reputation for being **curious**—but kittens take curiosity to the extreme! These young felines are eager to explore everything the world has to offer!

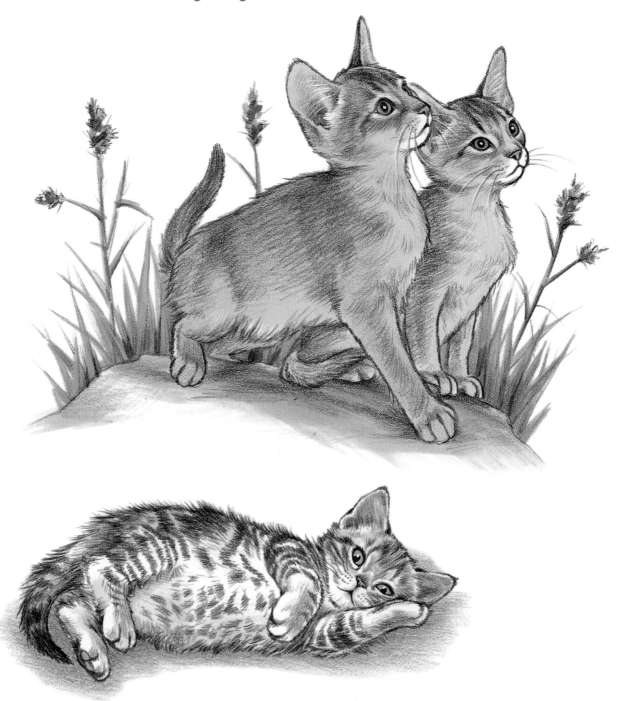

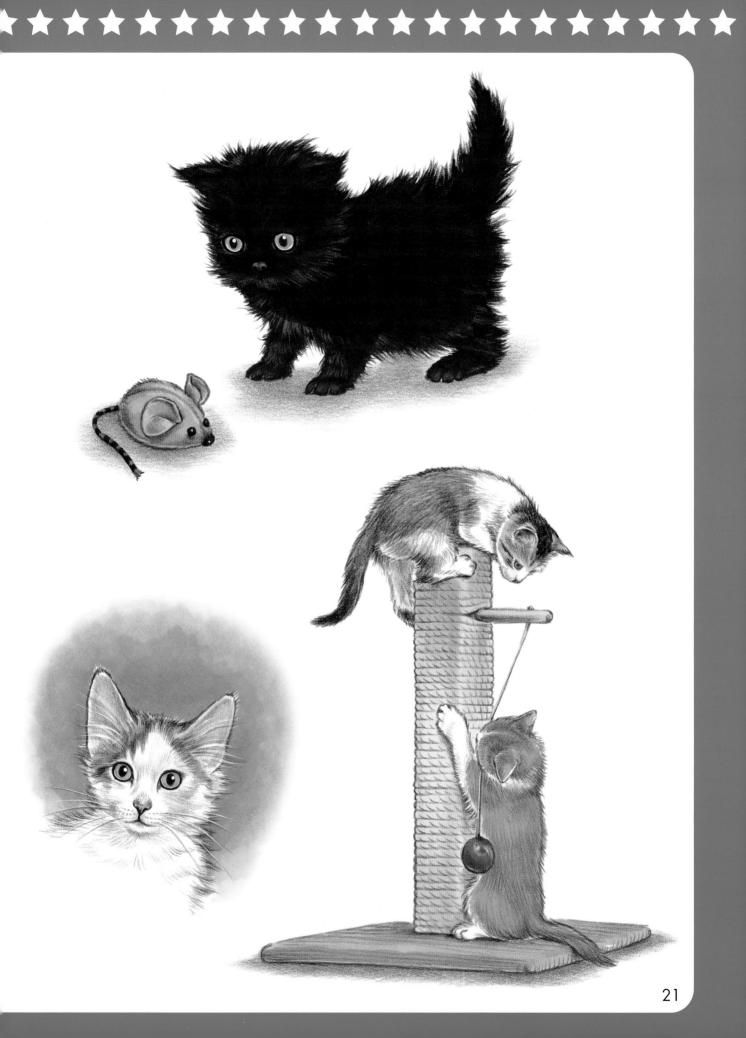

Turkish Angora

This **beautiful** breed has a **slender** body, a long neck, and a wedge-shaped head. The Turkish Angora is playful and devoted!

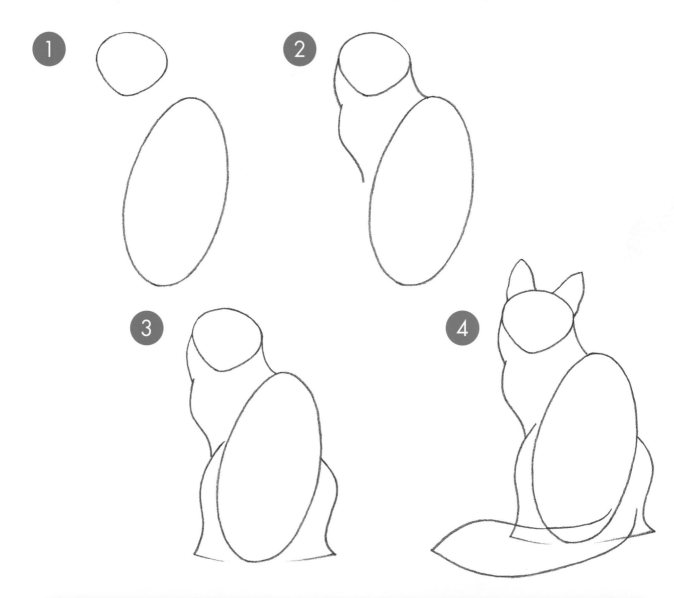

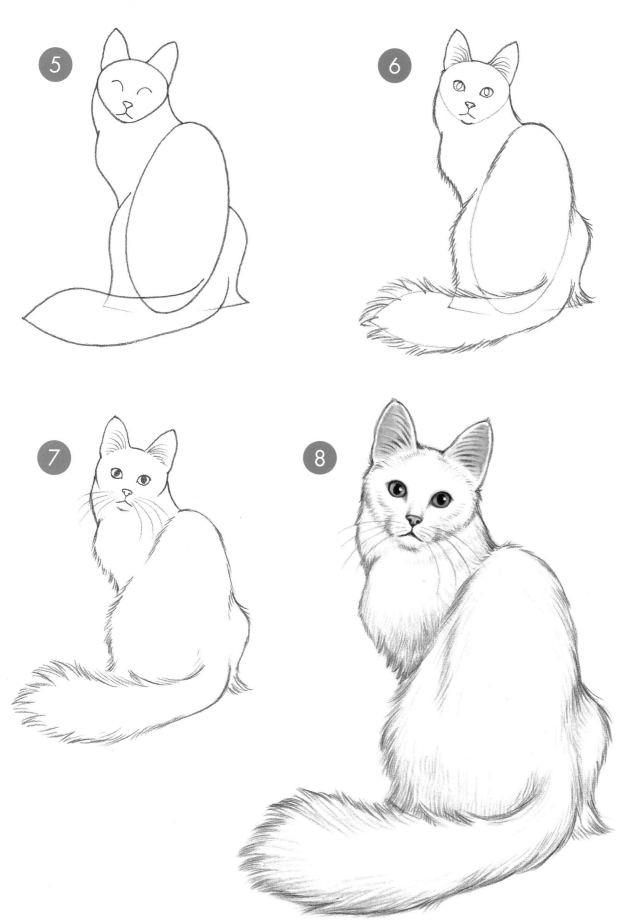

Russian Blue

Quiet-loving Blues can **happily** sit **still** for hours. To draw this cat in its comfy pose, begin with marshmallow shapes for its head and body.

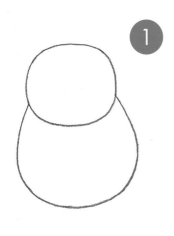

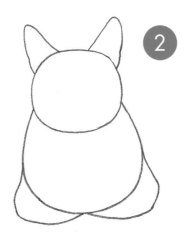

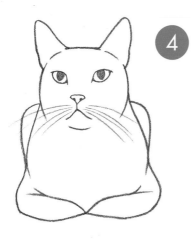

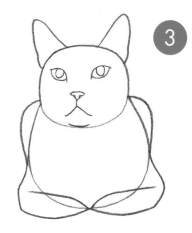

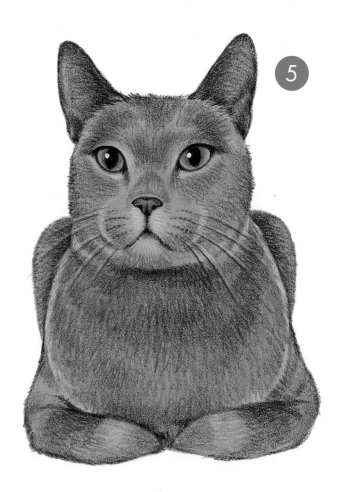

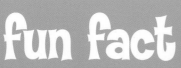
As you might guess from its name, the Russian Blue comes from Russia, where it was discovered by the British about 200 years ago. This breed has had many names in the past, including "Russian Shorthair," "Maltese Blue," "Archangel Blue," and "Foreign Blue."

American Curl

The **Curl** is the only breed to feature **ears** that curl backward.
It's a good thing this friendly feline loves to be center of attention!

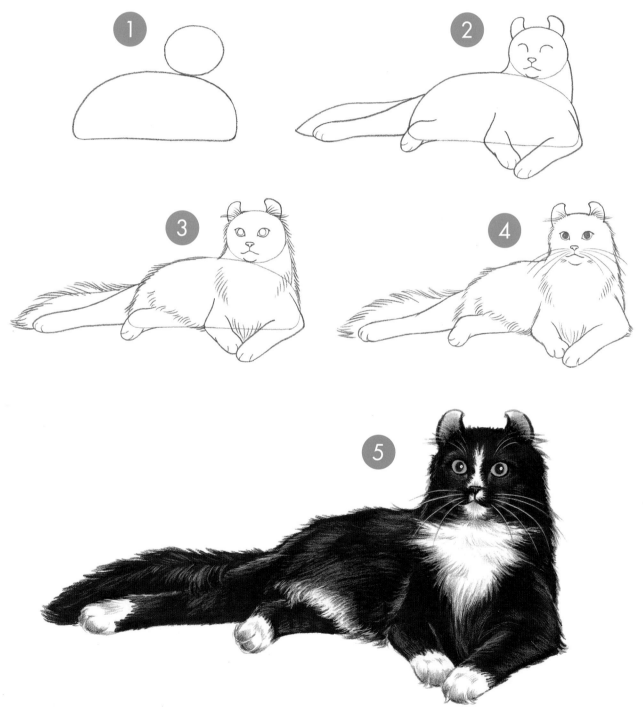

Norwegian Forest Cats

The Wegie is a **furry** feline with a thick, **heavy** coat of fur. Its mane and tail are fluffy, and its triangular ears are straight and tall!

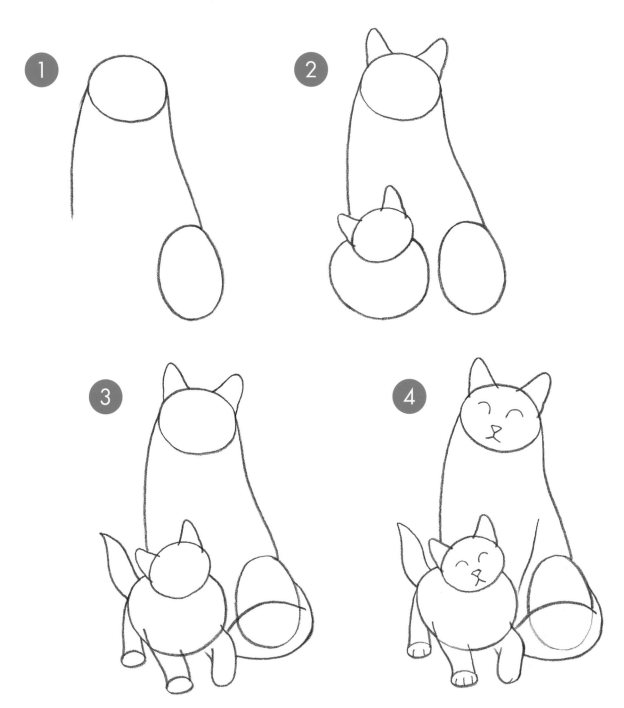

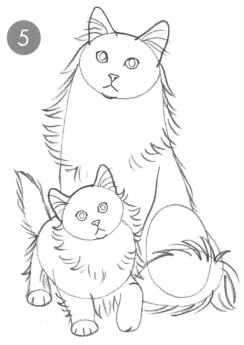

5

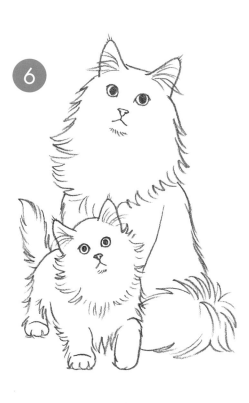

6

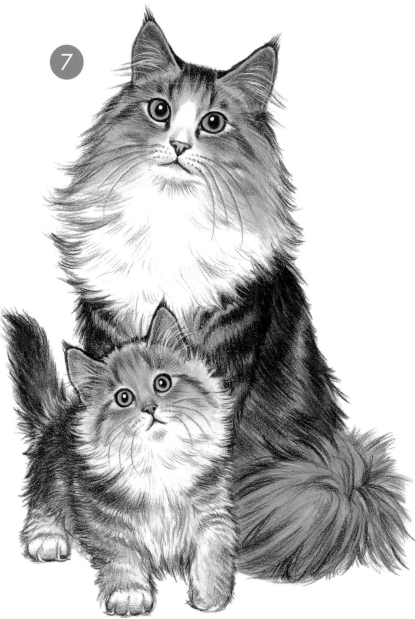

7

Scottish Fold

With unusual **flat**, folded **ears**, a round head, and big, golden eyes, the Scottish Fold looks like the feline version of an owl!

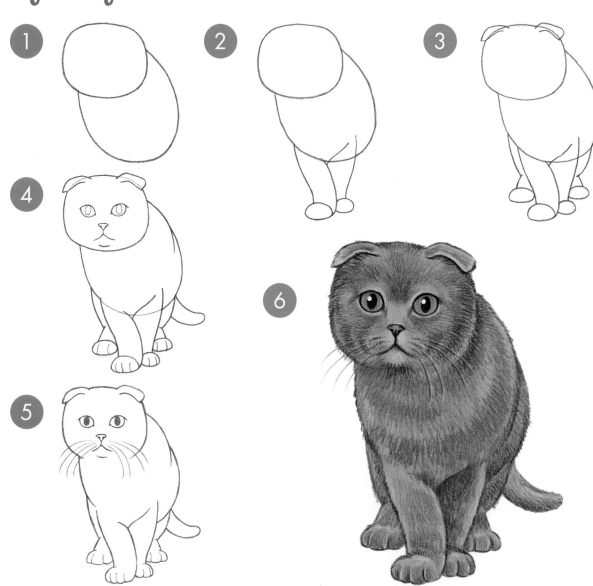

1

2

3

4

5

6

fun fact

Scottish Folds aren't bred with other Folds because their kittens can have crippling skeletal problems. To keep this breed healthy, Folds are mated with Scottish Straights (cats from the same bloodline without folded ears) and American or British Shorthairs.

Birman Kitten

The round **white paws** on this breed—also known as "The Sacred Cat of Burma"—distinguish it from other color-point varieties.

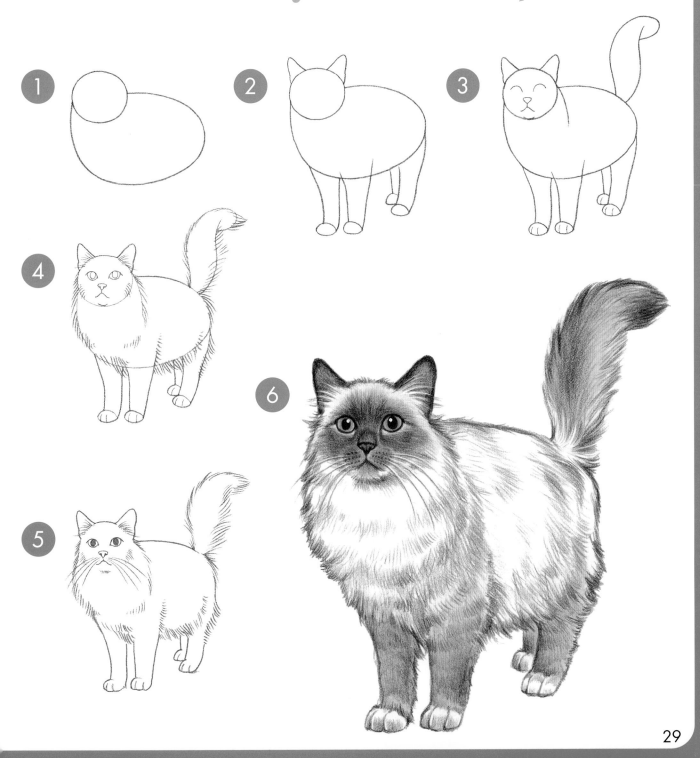

Traditional Siamese

This **"old-fashioned"** cat looks different than the triangular-headed Siamese, but both breed types are talkative and attention-loving.

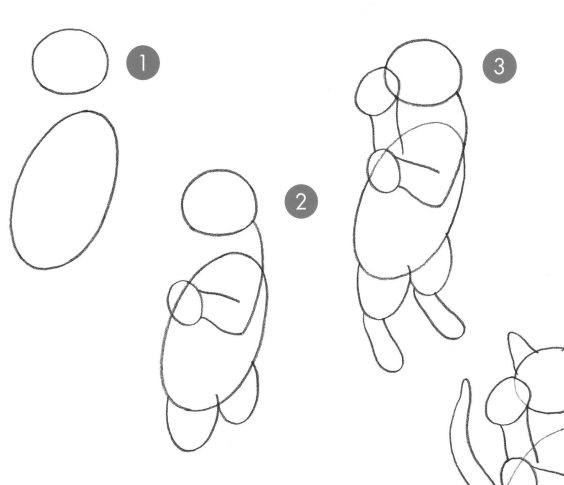

fun fact

The first Siamese cat to enter the United States was a gift to Lucy Hayes, wife of President Rutherford Hayes. But this wasn't the only Siamese to live in the White House! Jimmy Carter, Gerald Ford, and George W. Bush have all shared their headquarters with these elegant First Cats.

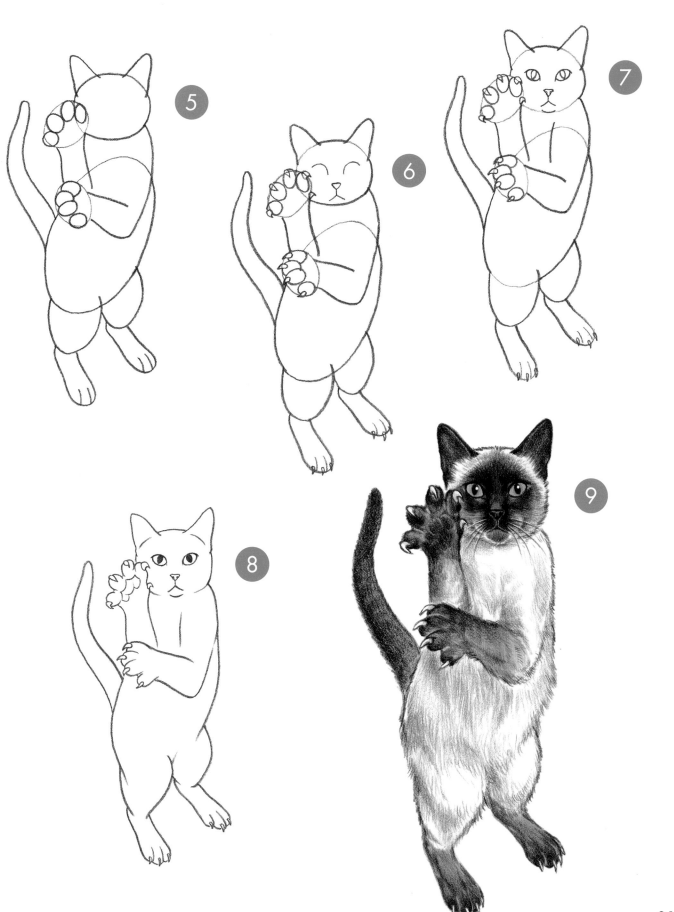

Japanese Bobtail

Most members of this **centuries-old** bobtail breed display a patched calico pattern called "mi-ke," which the Japanese consider lucky.

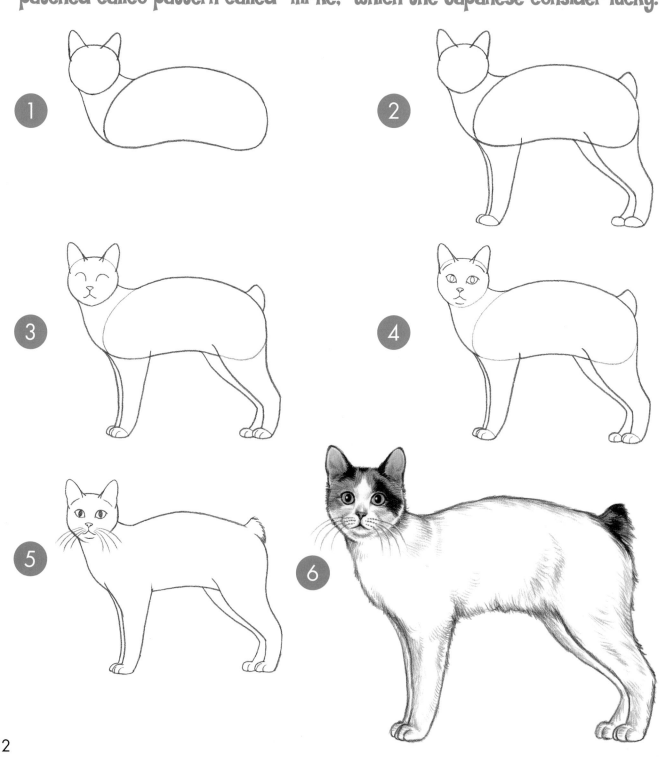

Sphynx

The huge, triangular **ears** of this **hairless** cat are hard to miss!
And its wrinkled skin, wide-set eyes, and large paws also draw attention.

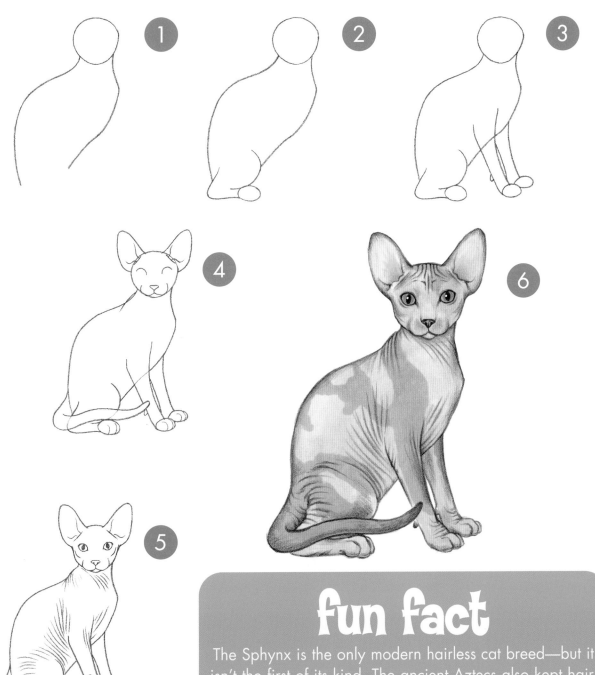

fun fact

The Sphynx is the only modern hairless cat breed—but it isn't the first of its kind. The ancient Aztecs also kept hairless cats; unfortunately, the Aztec breed is now extinct.

Somali

The **wild-looking** Somali is a long-haired version of the Abyssinian. This feline's coat is thickest at the ruff, haunches, and tail.

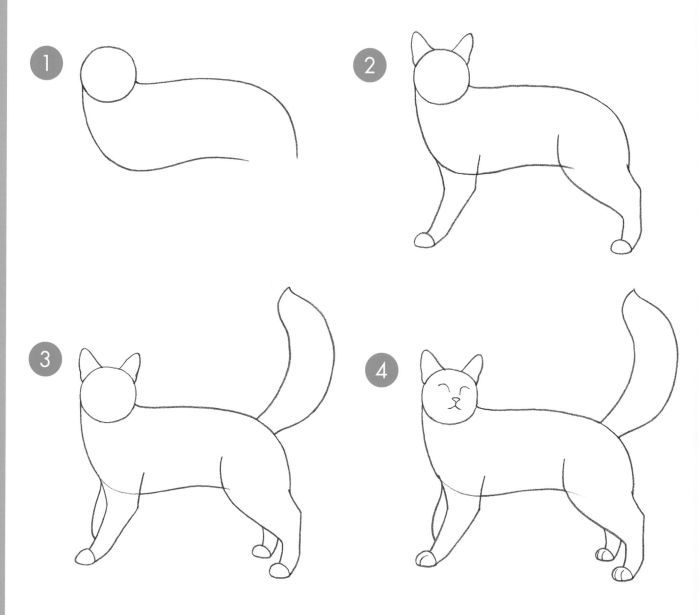

fun fact

The Somali's body shape, reddish-brown fur color, and full coat combine to make this cat look like another animal altogether. So it should come as no surprise that the Somali's nickname is "fox cat."

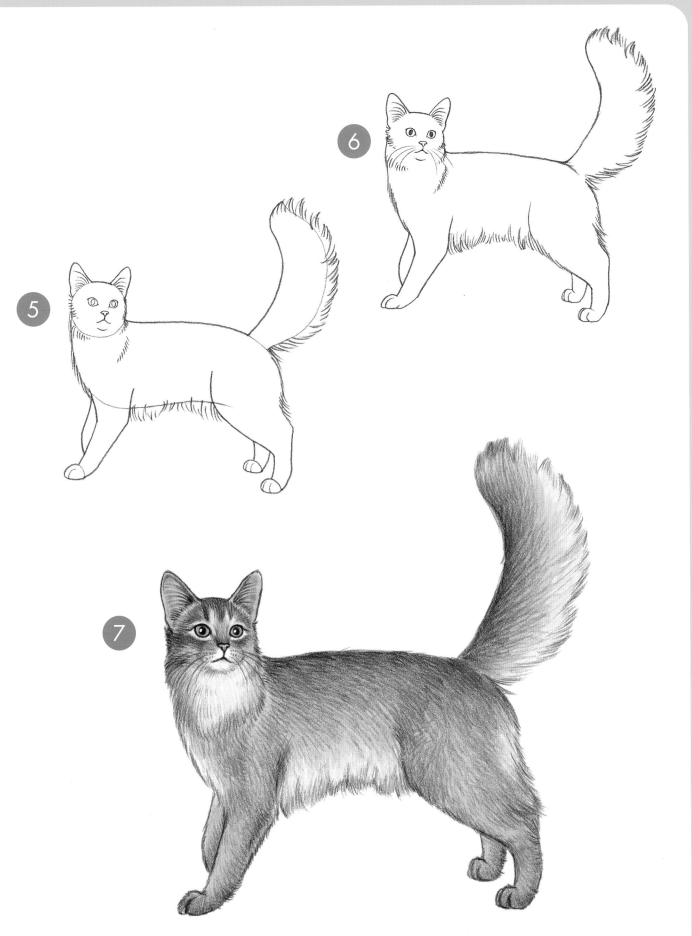

Persian Kitten

This **adorable**, pudgy-bodied, **sweet-faced** kitten is just one example of why Persians are the most popular cat in the world!

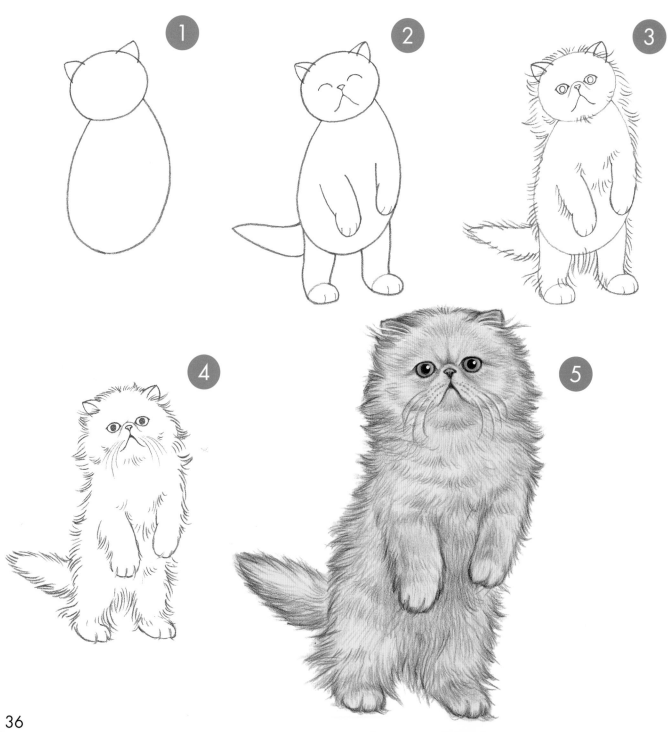

Devon Rex Kitten

You'd never guess by its **size,** but this **thin-bodied** breed loves to eat! This small kitty needs lots of food to fuel its active lifestyle.

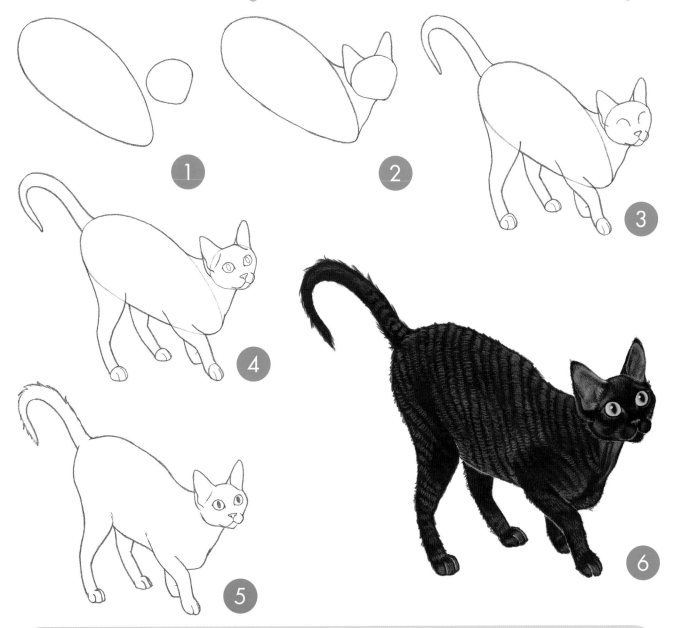

1

2

3

4

5

6

fun fact
The Cornish Rex and Devon Rex look similar—and, since they both have "Rex" in their name, people think they're related. But these cats come from two different bloodlines— if you mate the two, the kittens will have straight hair!

American Wirehair Kitten

A **coarse coat** is the most outstanding feature of this feline! Its short curls give this cat's fur a rough, wiry appearance.

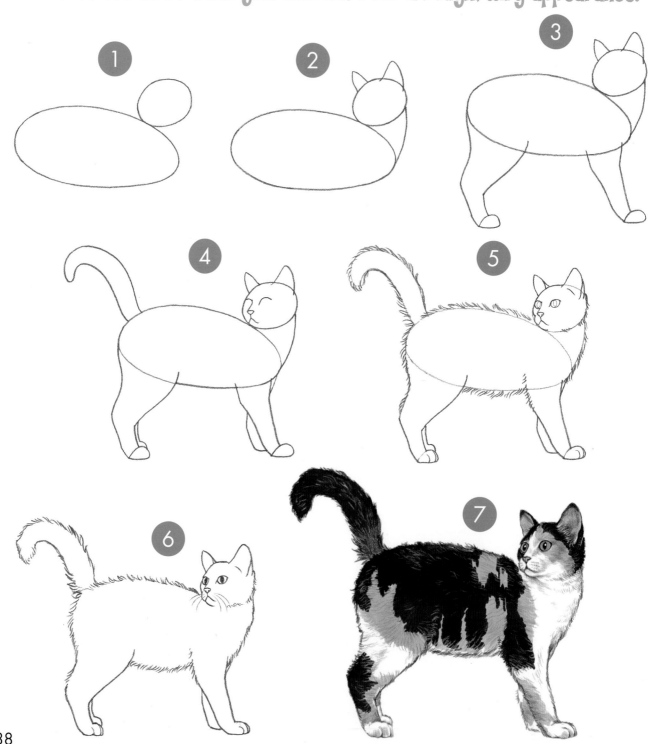

Exotic

The Exotic is a short-haired **version** of the **Persian.** Like its long-haired relatives, this cat hides a sweet nature behind a grumpy look!

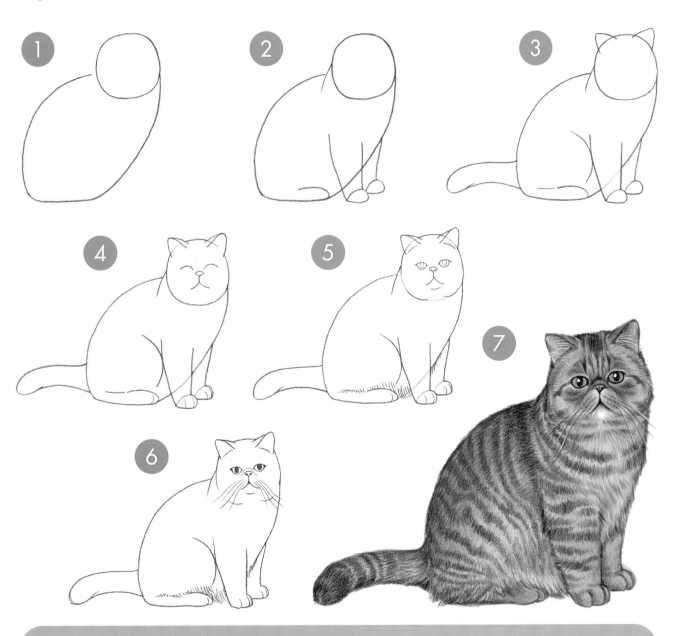

Korat

In Thailand, this **shiny-coated** cat is considered a symbol of good luck! The breed is also known for being vocal and affectionate.

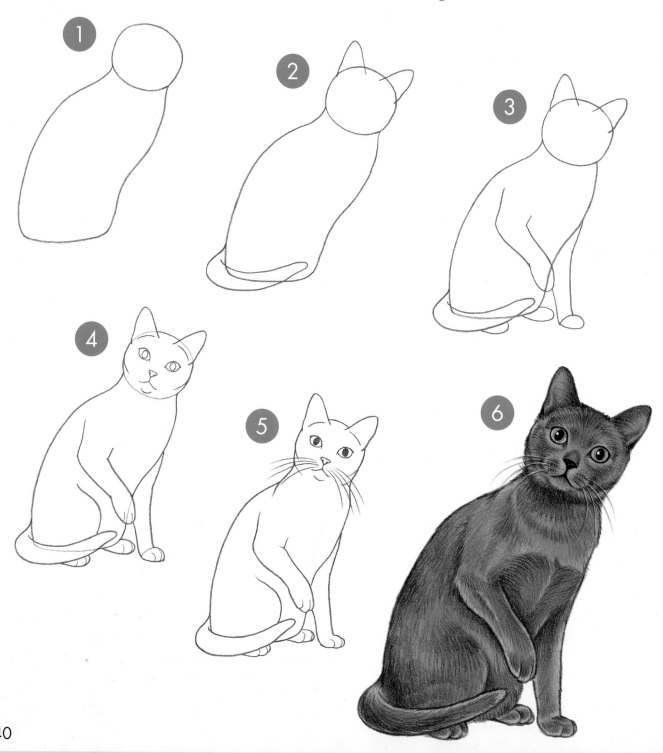